LC

MW01128299

~~BEGINNERS~~

The Complete Beginner's Step-by-Step Photo Guide to Loom Knitting Stitches and Techniques, and Knitting Inspiration Awesome Projects

JENNIFER FINN

Table of Contents

CHAPTER ONE

INTRODUCTION

You're probably already familiar with knitting on needles and weaving on a loom, but have you ever tried knitting on a loom? Not only is it possible, but loom knitting is also a quick and enjoyable way to create a variety of lovely knitted objects.

Loom knitting, which is easy on the hands, is a craft technique that involves the use of a loom rather than needles to make gorgeous knitted fabric that can be transformed into stunning homeware, fashion, and cozy accessories. While using a loom may appear to be a complicated process, loom knitting is surprisingly simple once you learn how, and is even suitable for children!

Knitting on a loom allows for the creation of the same types of projects as conventional knitting, including complicated motifs such as cables. The advantage of weaving these on a loom is that they are frequently easier on the hands and usually work up quickly.

Loom knitting dates back hundreds, if not thousands, of years. The most reliable information dates all the way back to the sixteenth century, when someone sought to develop an alternate manner of knitting and thus birthed a framed knitting "machine." If you've ever attempted finger knitting or spool knitting, you'll recognize the link, which may be how this larger version of loom knitting evolved.

CHAPTER TWO

THE KNITTING LOOM

What is a Knitting Loom?

The famous 'loom,' which simply refers to the ingenious apparatus used to weave yarn (or thread) together to create cloth, has numerous origins, ranging from medieval Europe to the complex craftwork of Amerindian tribes in the Americas.

Today, loom knitting is a recognized skill that can be used to create stunning wall hangings, caps, scarves, and blankets, among other things!

Loom knitting is particularly beneficial for people who have aching hands, such as those who suffer from arthritis or carpal tunnel syndrome. Additionally, it's an excellent alternative for people who want a needle-free approach to their projects, and the process is remarkably rapid, allowing you to whip up beautiful creations in record time. With a range of knitting looms and a wide variety of techniques available, loom knitting enables the creation of a wide variety of unique and stunning products. However, let us first discuss looms.

The Different Types of Knitting Looms

Knitting looms are available in a number of shapes, sizes, and materials and are referred to as a knitting board, rake, frame, or the classic loom. Some are fixed in their peg count, while others are changeable. Even better, you can create your own!

As with knitting needles, the size or gauge of your knitting is determined by the peg size and spacing on knitting looms. Larger pegs positioned further apart result in bulky or open knitting, while smaller pegs spaced closer together produce finer or tighter knitting.

Because each peg on a loom retains one stitch, the quantity of pegs also matters. You don't necessarily have to utilize every peg in a project, but you do need enough to accomplish the desired size of the knitted piece. To construct a blanket without putting numerous pieces together, for example, you would want a huge number of pegs, which are typically found on looms shaped like a giant S or figure 8.

Due to the critical nature of the loom size and shape to the outcome of the knitting, it is critical to ensure that you have the suitable loom for the job. Typically, patterns specify the type of loom to use, as well as the peg count and spacing. Additionally, it is critical to pay attention to the yarn weight advised for a pattern or loom, as well as whether more than one strand of yarn should be held together.

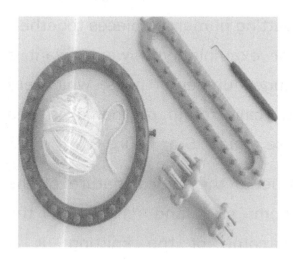

Selecting a Knitting Loom

There are numerous types of looms available, depending on the project at hand. While rake (long) looms are best suited for flat panel items such as blankets, circular looms are better suited for hats and cowls. The following are some of the looms you may encounter during your loom knitting trip!

Rake Looms

Rake looms, often referred to as long looms, have a single row of pegs and are typically used to construct flat panel products such as blankets and scarves using single knitting. When two rakes are placed parallel to one another, a knitting board is formed. Certain rake looms on the market feature two rows and an additional peg at either end, allowing for round weaving if needed. As with conventional knitting, fabric made on a simple rake loom will have a knit and purl side. The distance between the pins determines the gauge of the long knitting loom; hence, the closer the pins are together, the finer the knitted cloth!

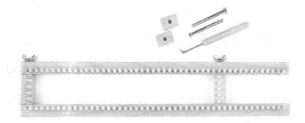

Circular and Various Round Looms

Round knitting looms, in contrast to their relative the rake, are looms that have no ending point. A round knitting loom is any device that allows continuous weaving; they come in a variety of fascinating forms and sizes, including circular, oval, square, triangular, and even heart-shaped looms. Due to the capacity to knit in the round, round loom knitting projects are frequently (but not solely) tubular in shape, which means that whether you're wanting to make socks, sleeves, or cowls, or anything else with a tube or circle shape, round looms are a must!

Afghan Looms

The serenity loom, also known as the S-loom, features an 'infinity' figure of eight construction and is ideal for creating vast panels of cloth that can be put together to create lovely afghans and blankets.

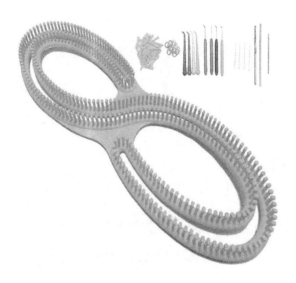

Sock Looms

Sock looms include an adjustable gauge, allowing you to quickly add (increases) and subtract (decreases) stitches to achieve the appropriate size for your entire family, whether you're knitting adult socks or baby booties.

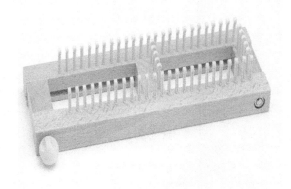

Weaving Loom

Loom weaving is a unique fiber craft from loom knitting. Unlike the knitting loom, the weaving loom lacks pegs and instead utilizes a number of bent threads as a framework for weaving in your yarn. The weaving loom is used to create exquisite wall hangings and tapestries.

15

CHAPTER THREE

HOW KNITTING LOOM WORKS

The majority of loom knitting is classified into three types: circular knitting, which results in a tube; single knitting, which results in a single panel; and double knitting, which results in a reversible, extremely thick cloth. This is made feasible by the use of several types of looms.

On your loom, you can create your favorite knitting stitches by wrapping the yarn around the pegs in a variety of ways. From classic stitches to more elaborate forms like lace or cable work, different wrapping techniques will yield diverse textures and designs to produce satisfyingly fluffy projects.

Single knitting can be done on any loom, however circular knitting necessitates the use of a continuous ring or peg frame. If you have a round loom and wish to create a flat (non-tube) piece of knitting, simply work back and forth on the pegs rather than in a circle.

Both single and circular knitting projects typically begin with an e-wrap cast on, in which the yarn is wrapped around each peg used in the project. Wrapping continues in the same manner as you add additional rows or rounds of stitches.

Double knitting is done on long looms with double rows of pegs. (Some have a peg at either end, allowing for circular knitting; however, these can also be used for single knitting). Double knitting begins with a figure eight cast-on, which involves wrapping the yarn back and forth across the rows of pegs as you knit.

When working with single and double knitting, you can alter the project size by working on only one side of the loom. This is more difficult to accomplish with circular knitting, which requires evenly placed pegs for each stitch.

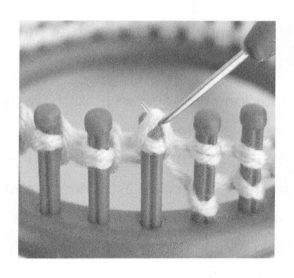

After winding the yarn around all
of the pegs once, proceed to do it
for a second time. Following that,
using a knitting hook (which most
looms include) raise the lower loop
of yarn up and over the peg,
leaving the top loop in place. This
is the end of a knit stitch.
Following the lifting of all the
bottom loops over the pegs, you

begin anew, encircling the pegs and creating new stitches.

Additionally, you can learn how to create additional stitches, such as standard purl stitches, loom-knitting-exclusive stitches, and cast-on and bind-off techniques, to create patterns and shapes in your work.

How to Use a Knitting Loom

Depending on the type of project you're working on, knitting looms come in a range of shapes and sizes. Long looms are great for scarves, while round (or circular) looms are best for caps, socks, and other crafts with a tube structure.

Pegs, Base, and Gauge

Let's get right to the point. The base, pegs, and gauge are the three main components of a loom's anatomy. The base of your loom is the frame at the bottom, which can be long or round and come in a variety of sizes. The pegs refer to the numerous short pins linked to the base, which are sometimes simply referred to as pins. The gauge is defined as the distance between each peg (or pin); the larger the gap between the pegs, the higher the gauge.

What Determines the Size of a Project?

Many factors influence the size of your project, the first of which is the size of your loom. Many inexperienced loom knitters refer to the loom's size in terms of pegs, but this is a huge no-no! It's vital to remember as a novice that the size of the foundation, rather than the number of pegs, dictates the size of your creation. The tension of your stitches, or how firmly your stitches are knit together, is influenced by the number of pegs and the gauge. More pegs does not always imply a larger size.

However, there is one exception, and that is the stitch style. If you use a loose stitch on your loom, such as an Ewrap stitch, your fabric will be looser and thus a somewhat larger size than if you used a garter stitch.

Rows vs. Peg Count

It's vital to keep in mind that the number of rows and pegs on your loom knitting project are not interchangeable. The number of rows dictates how many times you repeat the peg count, which determines the circumference or width of your project. If you're using a circular loom to make a tubular object like socks or a cap, the rows will only contribute to the length of the tube, and not the foot or head.

You'll also need a hook to catch and draw your yarn loops over to generate the knitted stitches, in addition to your loom and yarn.

Summary

Anatomy of a Knitting Loom

Before we get started, let's go over the different sections of the knitting loom to familiarize you with the terminology.

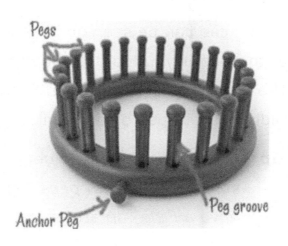

Pegs

Anchor Peg

Peg groove

Anchor Peg: Some knitting looms feature anchor pegs, whereas others do not. Don't worry if yours doesn't have one; you won't be missing out.

To keep the working yarn from unraveling of the pegs, wrap it around the anchor peg.

Pegs: Stitches are made by wrapping the yarn around the peg.

A little cap can be seen on the top of the peg if you look attentively. The little cap keeps the yarn from sliding off the peg by accident.

Tip: *If at all feasible, get a knitting loom with pegs that have a little cap at the top.*

Peg Groove: pegs with a groove are found on the majority of knitting looms. The groove makes it easy to knit off the loops.

CHAPTER FOUR

LOOM KNITTING STITCHES

Loom knitting, like needle knitting, offers a vast array of stitches for creating beautifully textured knitwear.

Before we get into individual stitches, there are two basic loom knitting methods: single knitting and double knitting.

Single Knitting

Single-knitting is the process of knitting stitches on pegs next to one another to create a cloth with a 'right' and 'wrong' side.

Knit Stitch (k)

The texture and appearance of a knit stitch made on a loom is identical to that of a knit stitch made with conventional needles. To make a knit stitch, tug on the yarn looped around your peg with your hook to form a new loop. To make a new knit stitch, lift the previous loop up and over and replace it with the new loop on your peg. That's all there is to it!

This is the most basic stitch, which may be paired with purl to make garter stitch or even ribbed stitches if mastered.

Flat Stitch (f)

Flat stitch is similar to knit stitch, however it is tighter and more compact. Simply stretch the working yarn across the top loop of the peg and raise the bottom loop over and off your peg with your hook, securing the working yarn in place by producing a new loop.

Purl Stitch (p)

The purl stitch is the inverse of the knit stitch; thus the backside of your fabric will be knit and the front side will be purl, just like in traditional knitting. As you learn to loom knit, both knit and purl stitches are wonderful starting places for launching you into a world of glorious textures and designs.

Double Knitting

If you're using a long loom, double-knitting is when you knit across two rails to create a front and back peg, giving you the same texture on both sides of the fabric.

No Wrap Stitch (nw)

This stitch is known as the basic knit stitch (k) when knitting with needles and as a flat (stockinette) stitch when knitting with looms. The no wrap stitch produces a robust yet beautifully versatile material that can be converted into fabulous accessories and homeware, similar to the gorgeous basic fabric made when knitting with needles. The no wrap stitch, as one of the most basic stitches, is a must-have for any loom knitter, and it may be done on a long or circular loom. That's all there is to it!

Ewrap (ew)

The ewrap, also known as the twisted stockinette stitch (tw St st) when knit with needles, looks great on both long and round looms.

Ribbing Stitch or Single Ribbed Stitch (rib)

The single ribbed pattern alternates ewrap threads with purl stitches on each row to create magnificent ridges of yarn, making it ideal for gloves and clothing with the classic ribbed effect.

CHAPTER FIVE

SINGLE KNITTING

Working neighboring pegs to create a single layer in flat panels or circular projects is known as single knitting. Stitch patterns and shapings can be achieved in a variety of ways.

This tutorial will walk you through the fundamentals of loom knitting step by step. I'll show you how to knit with a round loom here.

Although I'll be focusing on round knitting, the same knitting loom can be used to weave flat panels to make scarves, blankets, and even sweaters!

To begin, use a plain bulky weight wool yarn (or one that isn't textured) to make it simpler to see what's going on with the stitches. The photographs in this tutorial were taken with thick yarn. If you don't have any bulky weight yarn on hand, you can make do with the following:

- ✓ One strand of sport equals two strands of fingering (fine)
- ✓ Two sport (dk) strands equals one worsted strand
- ✓ One strand of bulky is equivalent to two strands of worsted equivalent (aran)

If you use different yarns, make sure to count all of the strands as one.

Gather the following materials for your first lesson:

- ✓ Knitting loom
- ✓ Tapestry needle
- ✓ Scissors
- ✓ Knitting tool

Let's get this party started!

We'll start by knitting a basic slip knot.

Slip Knot

1.   Form a circle with the working yarn, leaving a 5 inch beginning tail.

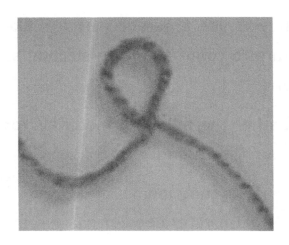

2. Fold the circle over the yarn from the skein.

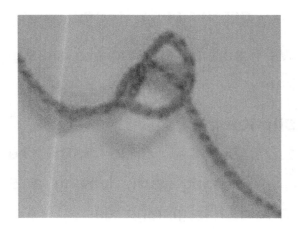

3. Grasp the yarn from the skein by reaching through the circle.

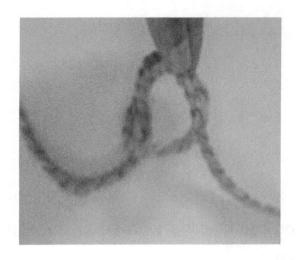

4. Tighten the noose on the knot by dragging the working yarn through the circle while gently pulling on the short end of the beginning yarn tail end.

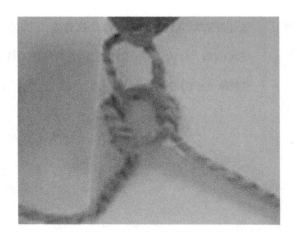

SlipKnot is finished.

The foundation row will be placed on the knitting loom after the slip knot.

Casting On

Casting on is the process of threading the knitting loom for the first time.

In this part, we'll go over two methods: the classic e-wrap and the chain cast-on methods.

E-wrap Cast On

When you need live stitches or a very flexible opening, this is the option to go with.

Form a slip knot with your working yarn before beginning your cast on. Start by tying a slip knot on your first peg (any peg can be your first peg).

1. With your right hand holding the working yarn and your left hand holding the loom. Bring the working yarn to the knitting loom's center.

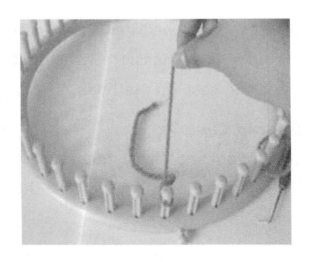

2. Wrap the yarn around the next peg that is not occupied. You can do this by:

    a. Moving around the peg in a counter-clockwise direction, if you are knitting clockwise around the loom

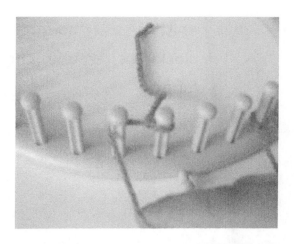

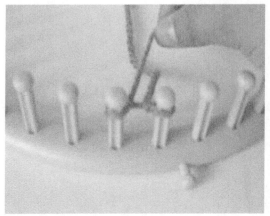

b.   Moving around the peg in a clockwise direction, if you are knitting counter-clockwise around the loom

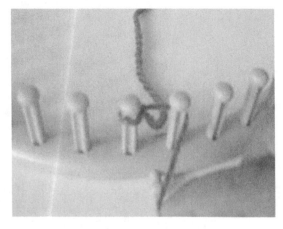

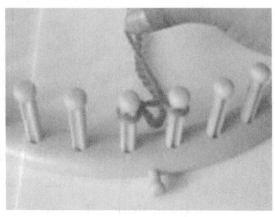

3   Continue in this pattern around the knitting loom. You're ready to start knitting on your loom when you reach the last peg.

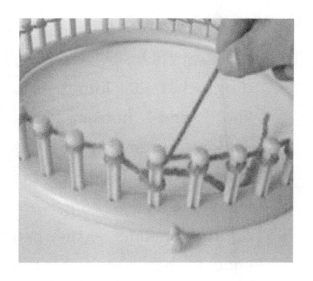

Chain Cast On

The Chain Cast On resembles the Cable Cast On in appearance.

Form a slip knot with your working yarn before beginning your cast-on. Start by tying a slip knot on your first peg (any peg can be your first peg). Take the working yarn towards the loom outside.

1. Make a chain by inserting the crochet hook into the slip knot and hooking the working yarn. Keep the chain on the inside of the loom and the working yarn on the outside – the peg should be between the working yarn and the chain.

2. Make a chain by hooking working yarn between pegs 2 and 3 and pulling it through the chain produced in Step 1 towards the inside of the loom. The working yarn should have wrapped around the peg outside.

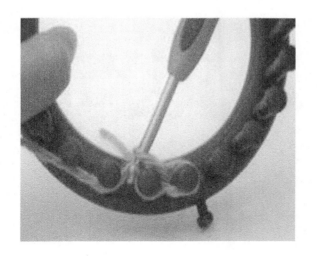

3.   Continue in this fashion around the loom, producing a chain around the peg. On the outside of the loom, the working yarn is located, while the chains are located on the inside.

Note:

- ✓ Always keep the working yarn on the outside of the loom
- ✓ Each peg has one loop attached to it
- ✓ Finish the circle by placing the last chain on the first peg. There will be two loops on the first peg

✓ Place the last chain on the last peg for a flat panel

Knitting on the Loom

You're ready to start knitting after your foundation row is on the knitting loom. The twisted knit stitch, the knit stitch, and the purl stitch are the three basic stitches we'll look at.

Twisted Knit Stitch

This stitch is made in the same way as the e-wrap cast-on method described above. This stitch is sometimes referred to as the twisted knit stitch or a back loop knit stitch in needle knitting.

Make sure you have your foundation row on the knitting

loom before you begin knitting. It's as simple as writing the cursive letter "e" to make a knit stitch.

1.   Take inside of the knitting loom, the working yarn (the yarn that came from the ball of yarn).

2. Wrap the yarn around the peg in a clockwise motion around the knitting loom.

3. Wrap all of the pegs with e-wrap. There should be two loops on each peg.

4. Lift the bottommost loop off the peg with your knitting tool and let it fall towards the inside of the knitting loom.

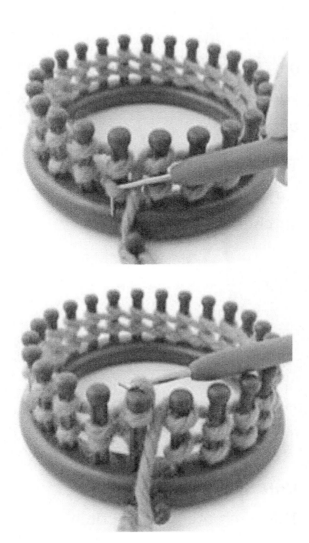

Tip: *Lift the bottommost strand on the last peg wrapped to keep your yarn from coming off the pegs.*

The twisted knit stitch looks similar to the image below. The stitches look like the letter y.

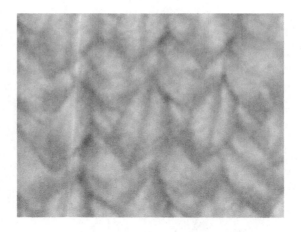

Knit Stitch

This creates a stitch that resembles the needle knit stitch.

The steps are as follows:

1. Position the working yarn in front of the peg and above the peg's loop.

2. Insert the knitting tool, working from the bottom up (behind the loop on the peg). Form a loop by catching the working yarn with the tool.

3.   Keep the freshly formed loop
      in your hand (the loop from
      Step 2).

4. Take the loop off the peg
    that was originally on it.

5. Place on the peg, the loop
    you're holding (the loop from
    step 3). To tighten the stitch,
    pull on the working yarn.

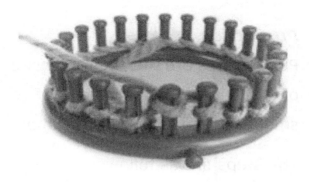

The knit stitch resembles the image below. The stitches are well-defined, resembling lowercase letters V.

Purl Stitch

Purl stitches are the polar opposite of knit stitches. Instead of a smooth V, the fabric will be lumpy.

The steps are as follows:

1. Position the working yarn in front of the peg and beneath the peg's loop.

2. Hook the working yarn with the tool by inserting it from the top down.

3.   Pull up through the stitch the loop caught with the tool. With your fingertips, hold it.

4.   Take the peg's original loop off.

5.   Place on the peg, the loop you're holding (the loop from step 3). To tighten the stitch, gently tug on the working yarn.

The purl stitch resembles the image below:

Flat Stitch (f)

The flat stitch is similar to the knit stitch in appearance; however it is the shortest and tightest stitch.

1.   Hold above the loop on the peg, the working yarn.

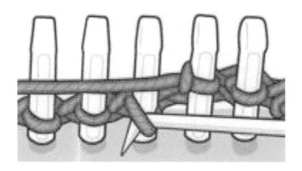

2. Lift the bottom loop over the peg and away from it. Then repeat on the next peg, and so on until all of the pegs have been knit.

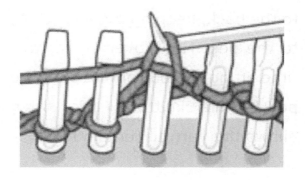

Tip

Hold the working yarn securely but loosely when knitting with the flat stitch. If you pull the working yarn too tight, the knitting will have a lot of tension and will be difficult to hook over.

U Stitch (u)

The U Stitch resembles the knit stitch but is a little tighter.

Bring the yarn to the front of the peg and wrap it around the loom to the back, keeping the yarn close to the peg. Hook over again, this time lifting the bottom loop off the peg. While knitting, this stitch allows the yarn to remain loose.

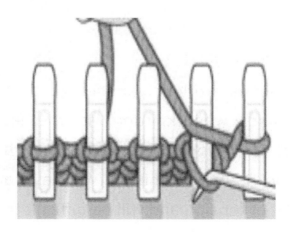

Increasing Stitches

By adding stitches to your knitting, you can make it wider. YO (yarn over) Increase and Make 1 (M1) are two ways for increasing stitches that have been suggested.

Note: *You can do this at one or both ends of your knitting.*

1. YO Increase on Edge

This simple method can be used if the edge of your knitting will be linked to another piece and the knit edge will not be visible. Simply ewrap the empty peg next to the last stitch to add a new stitch. Then, as you knit the row,

wrap the yarn once more to work
the first stitch.

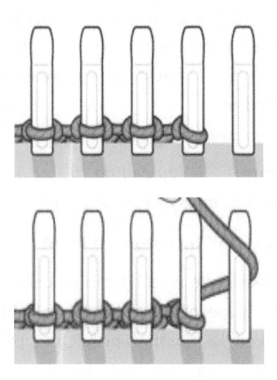

2.   Make 1 (M1)

This increase is made within a row
and results in a neat angled edge.
Move the last stitch to the empty

peg outward at the end of the row to add another stitch. Then, from behind the empty peg, catch the horizontal strand with the knit hook. It's the strand that connects one stitch to the next. Then place it on empty peg after twisting it in a clockwise direction.

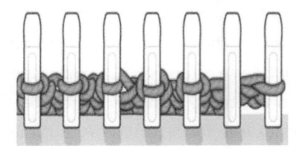

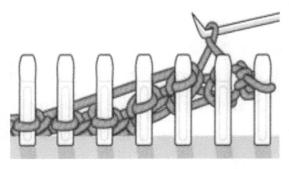

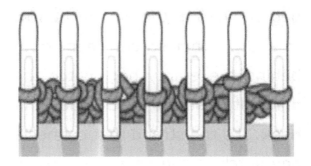

Note

Make 1L (left) or 1R (right) (right) will be used in some patterns. Twist the horizontal strand clockwise for M1L, and the horizontal strand counter-clockwise for M1R. Use M1L if the pattern does not state otherwise.

Decreasing Stitches

Reduce the number of stitches in your knitting to make it narrower. Knit 2 Together (K2tog) and Slip

Slip Knit (SSK) are two ways to decrease stitches that are recommended.

A.   Knit 2 together (k2tog)

Right slanting at the start of the row. To draw up, or decrease, stitches by half, you either execute one decrease or a sequence of decreases all the way across the loom. It's frequently used in hat knitting (crown decreases).

1.   Transfer the first stitch to peg 2, which will contain two loops.

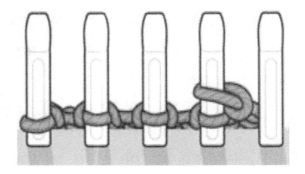

2.   Now it's time to work on the
     row. Take two bottom loops
     over the top loop when
     working the peg. This
     decreases by one stitch.

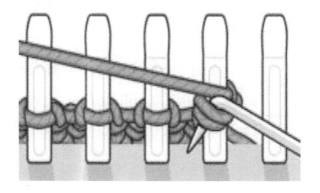

3. For a gathered decrease, k2tog across all stitches.

4. Remove all other loops and move to the left-hand neighboring peg.

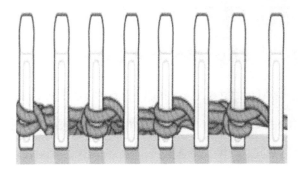

5. Then, to cover the empty pegs, move stitches inward. This will cut the number of stitches in half. Work 2 over 1 when knitting a row.

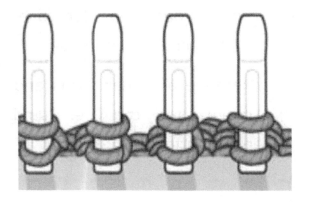

B.   Slip Slip Knit (SSK)

Slanting to the left. This reduction operates in the same way as the K2tog decrease; the difference being that it is left slanting. Transfer loop to peg 4 from peg 5. Lift the two bottom loops over one loop when working on peg 4. This decreases by one stitch.

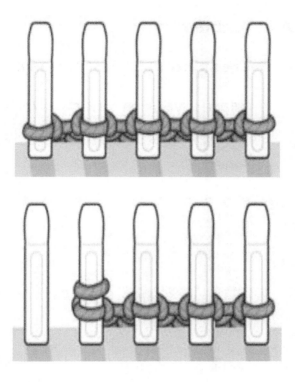

Cables Stitches

This pattern gives your knitting a rope-like twist. These can be done in many stitches. It's a good idea to use a cable needle or a stitch holder.

A.   Cables Over 2 Stitches

Left Crossing (LC-2 stitches)

1.   Place your working yarn behind peg 1 and skip this one.

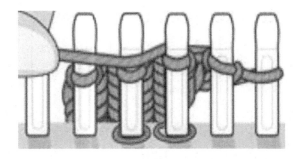

2.   Knit peg 2 and then insert a cable needle through it.

3. Next, transfer the stitch on peg 1 to peg 2.

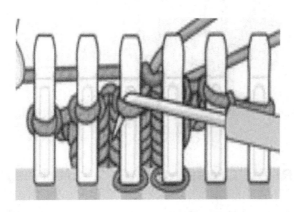

4. Place the stitch from the cable needle on peg 1 next.

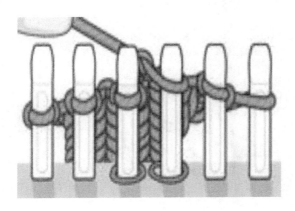

5.   And then knit peg 2.

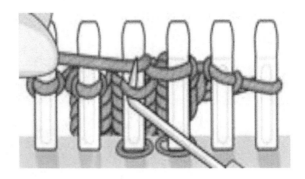

Right Crossing (RC–2 stitches)

1.   Hold stitch 1 to the center of
     the loom with a cable
     needle.

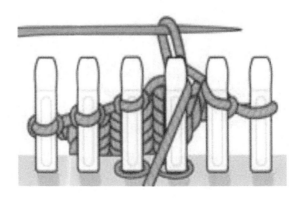

2. Knit peg 2 after moving the yarn to the front of it.

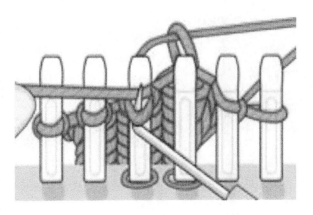

3. Transfer this stitch to peg 1 from peg 2.

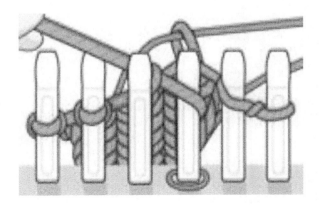

4. Next, remove the stitch from the cable needle and place it on peg 2.

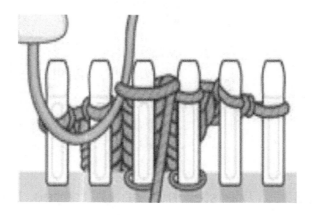

5. And then knit peg 2.

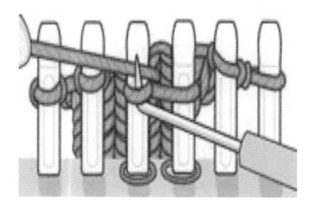

B.   Cables Over 3 Stitches

Crossing left (LC–3 stitches)

1.   Take the working yarn behind stitches 1 and 2, skipping those stitches.

2.   Put the freshly formed stitch on a cable needle, after working peg 3.

3.   Return to peg 1 and 2 and knit them.

4.   Transfer stitch from pegs 1 and 2 to pegs 2 and 3, respectively.

5.   Finally, place to peg 1 the stitch on cable needle.

Crossing right (RC–3 stitches)

1.   Thread a cable needle through the first stitch.

2.   Work stitches 2 and 3.

3.   Transfer stitch 2 on peg 1 and stitch 3 on peg 2.

4.   Then, on peg 3, place the stitch from the cable needle.

C.   Cables Over 4 Stitches

Crossing left (LC–4 stitches)

1.   Remove and put on a cable needle or stitch holder, stitches 1 and 2.

2.   Work stitches 3 and 4, and transfer them to pegs 1 and 2, respectively.

3. Place on to vacant pegs 3 and 4, the stitches from cable needle and work them.

4. Pull slack yarn gently to tighten cables.

Crossing right (RC–4 stitches)

1. Take the working yarn behind peg 1 and peg 2.

2. Work pegs 3 and 4, and put the stitches on a cable needle.

3. Work pegs 1 and 2 and move the stitches to pegs 3 and 4, respectively.

4. Remove stitches from cable needle and place them on pegs 1 and 2.

5.   Tighten each stitch's yarn
     slack.

CHAPTER SIX

SINGLE KNITTING BINDING OFF

It'll be time to remove your item from the knitting loom once you've mastered the basic stitches. The bind off is the procedure of detaching the piece from the knitting loom. The gather removal and the basic removal are the two forms of bind offs I'll look at.

The Gather Removal

The gather removal cinches the item's end together. When building a hat or any other object that requires one of the ends to be closed, this is the bind off to use.

You'll need your tapestry needle at this time. Leave around a 24-inch tail when cutting the working yarn. The yarn should be threaded through the tapestry needle.

The steps are as follows:

1.   Locate the working yarn on the peg to the left. Insert, through the stitch on the peg, the tapestry needle. (Yarn is displayed in various colors to show the steps.)

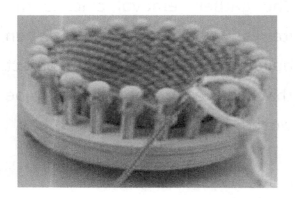

2.   * The yarn should be pulled through, and then the tapestry needle should be inserted through the stitch on the next peg. Repeat from * until all of the loops are on the yarn. Pass the tapestry needle through the first stitch once more when you reach the last peg in the round.

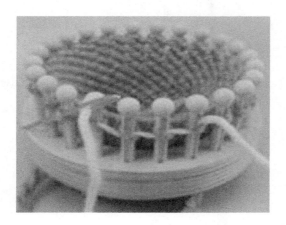

3.   Pop-off all of the pegs using your knitting tool. Gently tug on the yarn, securing the top tightly.

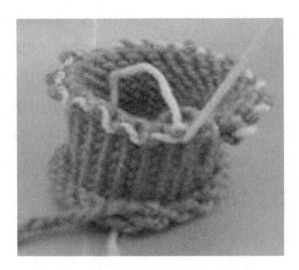

4.   Pass the tapestry needle through the top of the hat's center.

5.   Next, turn the hat inside out.
     Find the tapestry needle you
     left in Step 5 and make a
     series of crosses in the small
     hole at the top of the hat to
     close it. Make a small knot in
     the working yarn and snip it,
     leaving a 5 inch tail. And
     then weave in the ends.

The Basic Bind Off (Flat Removal Method)

For most knits, it's a decent general bind off approach. It is utilized when an open end is required. When removing items with an opening, such as sleeves, the flat removal method is utilized.

1. Knit the piece until each peg has only one loop. The last peg is where the working yarn comes from. Knit the first two stitches. Transfer the loop from the second to the first peg. Knit over. (The first stitch has been bound off). Transfer the stitch from

the first peg to the now-vacant second peg.

Knit the first two stitches:

After knitting the first two stitches

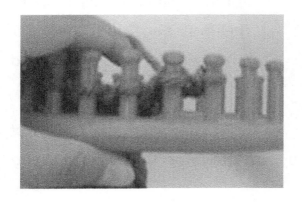

Move over to the first peg knitted, the loop from the second peg

2. Proceed to knit the next stitch. Transfer this loop to the first peg, and knit over (the second stitch is bound off).

Moving the stitch from the first peg to the unoccupied second peg

3.   Continue with Step 2 until all stitches are bound off.

4.   When you reach the final peg, cut the working yarn, leaving a 5-inch tail. And then knit the stitch in place. Take the stitch out of the peg. Pull the tail end of the yarn through the loop.

Thread the yarn tail end through a tapestry needle and slide it through the first stitch if binding off a tube. Weave the ends in.

CHAPTER SEVEN

DOUBLE KNITTING

Double-knitting on a loom produces a two-sided fabric with two rows of pegs and weaving that runs across both rows. This results in a knit that is finished on both sides, which is ideal for multi-color designs.

Cast On

Stockinette Cast On

1.   Work from left to right, starting with a slipknot on the first peg at the left side of the board (furthest away from you). If you're left-handed, you might wish to start from the right and work

your way left. Weave around the pegs, wrapping every other peg proceeding across the two rows of pins.

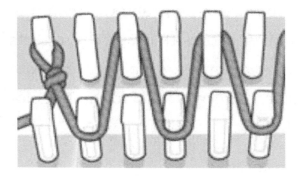

2.   When you reach the end of the loom, or the working section, bring the yarn straight over the end, flip the loom about, and weave back, wrapping around the pegs you missed the first time. You'll finish this

weaving by working down
and then back up to wrap all
of the pins.

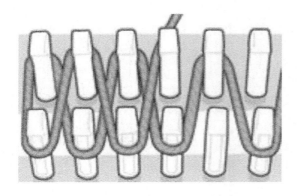

3. Secure the stitches by
    setting anchor yarn, which
    will also assist with moving
    the first few rows below the
    boards with it. A leftover
    piece of yarn roughly three
    times the length of your
    stitches serves as the anchor
    yarn. It should only be laid

across the stitches, with the ends dangling below the boards.

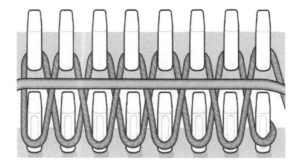

4. Repeat the wrapping technique with the anchor yarn until each pin has two loops. Then, with the bottom loop over the top loop, hook over. Make sure to work all pins on both boards and do this on both sides of the loom.

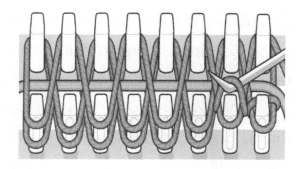

Figure 8 Cast On

When compared to the Stockinette Cast On, this method produces a much looser edging. Because you wrap both pins of each stitch at the same time, you only need to wrap the pins once with this type of cast on.

Begin at the left end of the board at your first stitch and the slip knot on the top pin. Wrap the opposite pin in a figure 8 pattern, then repeat around the same pins. Then wrap figure 8 around the next two pegs. Continue along the loom in this manner until all pegs have two loops. On both sides of the knitting board, hook bottom loop over top loop. You're now ready to start stitching your pattern.

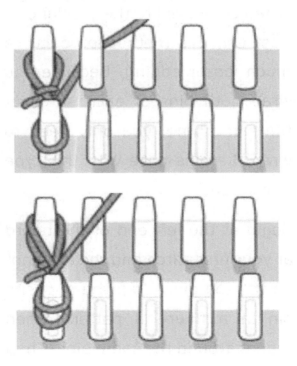

Bind Off

Bind Off Double Knit

Remove the stitches from the loom or the board.

Crochet Bind Off

1.   Starting at the opposite end of the yarn tail, lift off the first loop on the back board with your crochet hook.

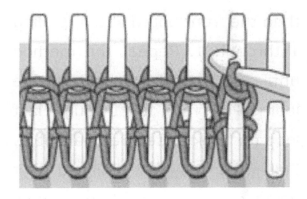

2.   Then, on the front board, pick up the first loop. Pull

through the back loop, the front loop on the hook.

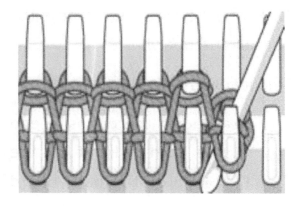

Pick up the next back board stitch, then the front board stitch, pulling 1 through 1. Repeat the method until you reach the end of the loom. Pull yarn tail through last loop on hook to secure final stitch. Pull yarn tail into finished knit using crochet hook. Your double knit piece is now complete.

Bind Off Anchor Yarn

If your design specifies that the anchor yarn be left in the knitted piece, such as in a cap, make sure you follow the pattern directions.

The bind-off gives your cast-on stitches a nice finished edge and allows you to remove the anchor yarn.

1. Begin at the opposite end of the yarn tail. Use your crochet hook to complete the project. Using a crochet hook, pick the first two loops.

2. Pull the loop closest to the
    hook through the opposite
    loop. Pick up each additional
    loop until you reach the end.
    Pull the yarn tail through the
    last loop on the crochet hook
    to secure the knot. Using a
    crochet hook, tuck the yarn
    tail into the finished knit.
    Remove anchor yarn from
    knitwear with care, and your
    knitted piece is finished.

There's no need to use double-knit to block the piece.

Knitting on the Loom

Stockinette Stitch

This stitch is made in the same way as the Stockinette Cast-On. It produces a uniform, smooth knit pattern.

1.   Weaving from front to back, start by wrapping the first pin on the top board and working your way down to the second pin on the bottom. Wrap every other pin all the way to the end of the row.

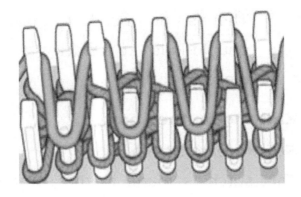

2.   Turn the board around and
      weave the yarn around both
      end pins and the open pins.
      You'll continue to weave in
      the pattern of "every other
      pin." All of the pins in the
      row should be hooked over.

Note

From each side edge, hook over to
the center, left end to center, and
right end to center. The edges will
be more equal as a result of this.

Repeat row after row with this hook, but change the center point to avoid a center line in the knitting.

Ribbing Stitch

This stitch looks fantastic on cuffs, hems, and turtlenecks. This stitch is similar to stockinette; however it is done at an angle. Start with an even number of stitches and work your way up.

1. Begin weaving from the first pin on the top board and work your way down to the third pin on the bottom board, weaving every other pin until you reach the end.

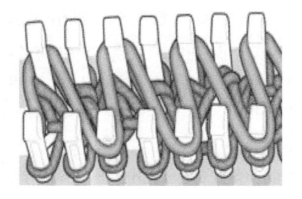

2. At the end of the board, there will be two consecutive pins that require a wrap; this is right.

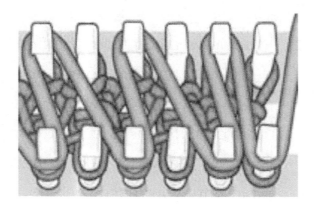

3. Rotate the board and wrap every other pin again, one by one, from 1 to 3. You're now wrapping in the opposite direction. This is how the ribbing is made. Make certain that all pins are wrapped. To finish the row, hook over all of the pins.

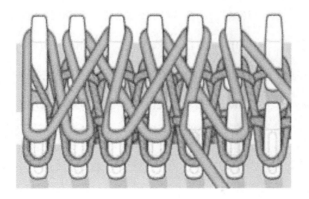

Criss Cross (2 Weave Patterns)

Alternate the following two weaving patterns to make the Criss Cross Stitch.

Weaving Pattern 1

Note: White yarn is used to show the weaving pattern.

1. Bring the yarn down to the lower 4th needle from the top 1st needle. Skip every other needle as you weave the yarn across the boards.

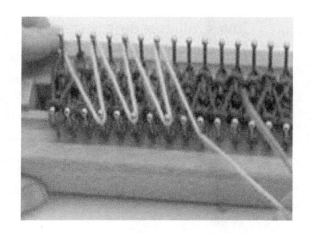

2. Bring the yarn straight across the end needles at the board's end.

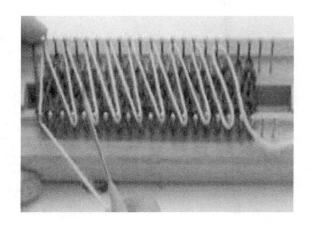

3. Cover all needles, wrapping back to the beginning.

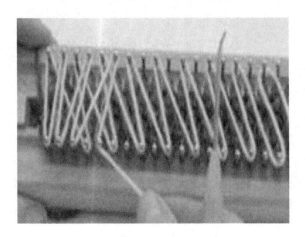

4. Hook over all of the needles.

Weaving Pattern 2

1. Begin at needle 1 on the back board and work your way down to needle 3 on the front board. The yarn should then be weaved back to needle 2 on the top board and down to needle 5 on the front board.

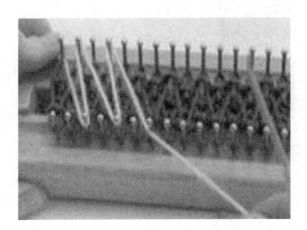

2. Weave every other needle to the end of the board from

here. The last two needles will be in a row (i.e. will be consecutive). Take the yarn straight across the top board at the end of the row. And then turn the board around.

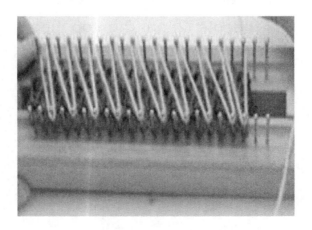

3. Cover all needles to the beginning of the board. Hook over all of the needles.

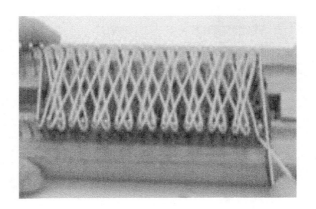

Loopy Rib Stitch

The Loopy Rib has a smooth and open feel about it. This yarn is perfect for shawls, scarves, and afghans.

The steps are as follows:

1.   Begin with a huge loop knot.
        Slip over the first two
        needles on the upper (or
        top) board.

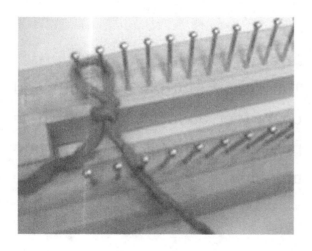

2.   Bring the yarn all the way
        down to needle 4 on the
        bottom board or the board
        nearest to you. In a counter-

clockwise fashion, wrap around needles 4 and 3.

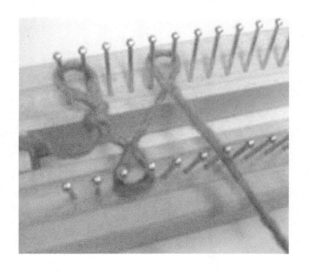

3.   Wrap sets of two needles continuously, alternating the boards and skipping two needles in between. Around the needles, the wraps should form a circle while in the middle of the boards,

they should make a giant X pattern.

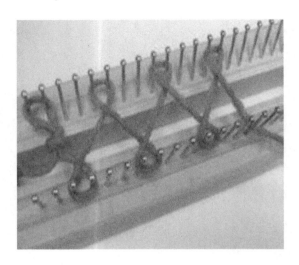

4.   When you reach the end of the board, make a circle around the last two needles. You'll wrap around the outside, come straight across the inside, and then wrap around the opposite set of two needles.

5. For a full circular, continue wrapping back to the starting point.

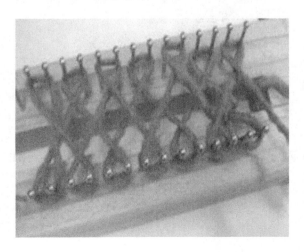

6.   Layover the weaving the anchor yarn. Repeat the circular pattern all the way around the board until you have the same number of loops.

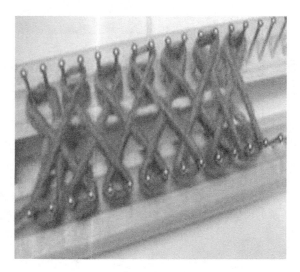

7.   On all set of two needles, lift the bottom big loop.

8. Pull down on anchor yarn after hooking all large loops. Over the sets of two needles, weave the same pattern. For each row, repeat the wrap, and hook over.

Zigzag Stitch

It creates a lovely afghan or sweater cuff or border. Scarves and hats can also be finished with it.

The steps are as follows:

1. Only one pass down the board is required for this stitch. Begin by wrapping your yarn around the first

three needles consecutively, front to back. Return to needle 1 on the opposite board after wrapping the three needles.

2.   Wrap all needles at this angle, back and forth over all needles, until they are covered. One half of the board will be overlapping, resulting in a double amount

of wraps on the first three
needles on that side.

3.   When you reach the end,
     one side of the board will be
     filled, while the other will
     have three empty needles.
     Wrap the remaining three
     needles consecutively, back
     to front, starting with needle

3. This will result in a board overlap on one side.

4. Due to the continuous wrap to cover all needles, one side of both ends of the board has an overlap.

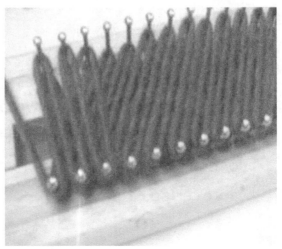

5. All stitches should be hooked.

The initial row of the Zigzag will differ slightly from the subsequent rows.

Due to the overlap, the first three needles on one side will have three wraps instead of just two. Make sure to leave two loops by lifting only the bottom loop while doing these needles.

6.   Lift the bottom loop over the top of the needle on all other needles with 2 loops to leave 1 loop on all needles.

7.   The last three stitches on the
      second row of this stitch
      (and all others) will all have
      three loops. Lift 1 and leave
      2 loops if hooking the side
      with the overlap.

      Lift over two loops and leave
      only one loop on the needle
      if hooking the side (as seen
      in photo below) without the
      overlap.

      **If it has the overlap, lift 1
      and leave 2 loops on the
      needle when hooking the
      first 3 needles for rows
      2+.**

Lift two bottom loops and leave one loop on the needle if it does not have the overlap (as seen in the picture below).

Lift 1 loop over needle and leave 1 loop on needle for all other needles.

Increasing and Decreasing

Increasing

By adding stitches to your knitting, you can make it wider. On the loom, you can add additional stitches at the side edges or inside the row.

1.   Transfer the preceding stitch from the back board's first peg to the adjacent empty peg.

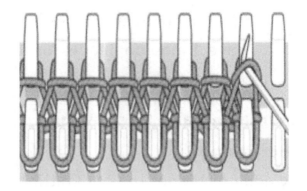

2. Transfer the previous stitch from the front board to the vacant peg adjacent to it. You've added one stitch to your knitting.

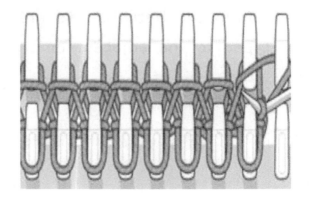

To increase the knitting at additional spots on the knitted piece, move the stitches out to one or both sides, leaving empty pins where the increase will take place. Create the new stitch by picking up the previous row stitch from an adjacent stitch and placing it on the empty pin once all the loops have been shifted to expose the empty pins. Before beginning the project, make sure you have enough empty pins on your knitting board to allow for the increase in stitches.

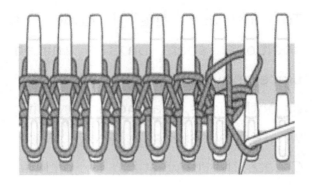

Note

If desired, increase in one row from both ends of the boards, resulting in a 2-stitch increase in knitting.

Decreasing

Reduce the number of stitches in your knitting to make it narrower. Reduce the number of stitches and shape your knitting by decreasing at each end of your loom, in the middle, or anyplace along the way.

An empty pin will be created by knitting two stitches together. The stitches will then shift over to close the empty pins, working a reduced number of stitches in the process. This can be done whenever necessary or as directed by the pattern.

1.   Transfer stitch from the required peg (say peg 3) to the back board's adjacent peg. Peg 3 is currently completely vacant.

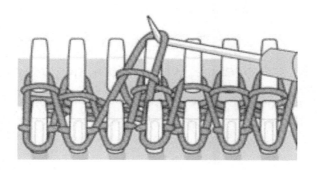

2.	Then, on the front board, move the identical stitch to the adjacent peg.

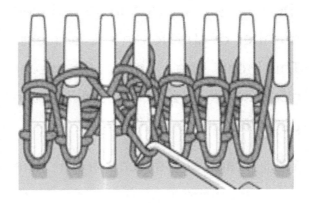

3.	Fill in the vacant pins with the outside stitches. Knitting is now reduced by one stitch. Make sure to work the peg with 2 stitches as 2 loops over 1 when hooking over the next row.

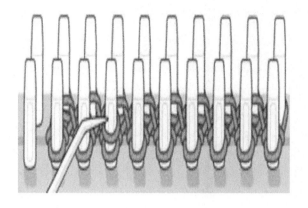

Knitting Ideas

With your new knitting looms, here are some ideas on what you can do: hats, soap sacks, slippers, and bags, etc.

ENJOY!!

Made in the USA
Coppell, TX
28 October 2024

39331414R00079